Wendell Phillips

Disunion:

Two Discourses at Music Hall, on January 20th, and February 17th, 1861

Wendell Phillips

Disunion:
Two Discourses at Music Hall, on January 20th, and February 17th, 1861

ISBN/EAN: 9783337086466

Printed in Europe, USA, Canada, Australia, Japan

Cover: Foto ©ninafisch / pixelio.de

More available books at **www.hansebooks.com**

TWO DISCOURSES AT MUSIC HALL,

On January 20th, and February 17th, 1861.

BY

WENDELL PHILLIPS.

"If the sovereignty of the Union were to engage in a struggle with that of the States, at the present day, its defeat may be confidently predicted; and it is not probable that such a struggle would be seriously undertaken. As often as steady resistance is offered to the Federal Government, it will be found to yield. Experience has shown that whenever a State has demanded any thing with perseverance and resolution, it has invariably succeeded; and that if a separate Government has distinctly refused to act, it was left to do as it thought fit."—DE TOCQUEVILLE, in 1834.

———————

BOSTON:

PUBLISHED BY ROBERT F. WALLCUT,

No. 221 WASHINGTON STREET,

1861.

THE LESSON OF THE HOUR.

THE office of the pulpit is to teach men their duty. Wherever men's thoughts influence their laws, it is the duty of the pulpit to preach politics. If it were possible to conceive of a community whose opinions had no influence on their government, there the pulpit would have no occasion to talk of government. I never heard or knew of such a community. Though sheltered by Roman despotism, Herod and the chief priests abstained from this and that because they " feared the people." The Sultan dared to murder his Janissaries only when the streets came to hate them as much as he did. The Czar, at the head of a government whose constitution knows no check, but poison and the dagger, yet feels the pressure of public opinion. Certainly, where pews are full of voters, no question but the sermon should be full of politics.

"The Lord reigneth ; let the earth rejoice." "The Covenant with Death" is annulled; "the Agreement with Hell" is broken to pieces. The chain which has held the slave system since 1787 is parted. Thirty years ago, Southern leaders, sixteen years ago, Northern Abolitionists, announced their purpose to seek the dissolution of the American Union. Who dreamed that success would come so soon? South Carolina, bankrupt, alone, with a hundred thousand more slaves than whites, four blacks to three whites, within her borders, flings her gauntlet at the feet of twenty-five millions of people in defence of an idea, to maintain what she thinks her right. I would New England could count one State as fearless among her six! Call it not the madness of an engineer who stands in front of his cannon at the moment of discharge ; — call it rather the forlorn hope of the mariner, seizing plank or spar in the fury of the storm.

The mistake of South Carolina is, she fancies there is more chance of saving slavery outside of the Union than inside. Three States have followed her example. Probably the rest of the Slave States, or many of them, will find themselves unable to resist the infection, and then the whole merciless conspiracy of 1787 is ended, and timid men will dare to hate slavery without trembling for bread or life.

Let us look at the country — the North, the South, and the Government. The South divided into three sections: 1st, Those who hold slaves exactly as they do bank-stock or land — and of course love the Union, which enables them to treat man as property — timid wealth shrinking from change, but so timid as to stand dumb. 2d, Those who have ruled the nation sixty years, monopolizing Presidents' chairs and embassies; defeated now, these plan, in earnest sincerity, for another nation with presidencies and embassies all to themselves. 3d, A class made up from these two, who cling to the Union in their hearts, but threaten loudly, well knowing the loudest threats get the best bargain.

The object of the South is a separate confederacy, hoping they can stand long enough for the North to ask for annexation on their terms.

Then comes the Government, so-called — in reality a conspiracy against justice and honest men; some of its members pilferers and some traitors — the rest pilferers and traitors too. Like all outgoing administrations, they have no wish to lessen the troubles of their successors by curing the nation's hurt — rather aggravate it. They have done all the mischief in their power, and long now only to hear the clock strike twelve on the 4th day of March.

Then look at the North, divided into three sections. 1st, The defeated minority, glad of any thing that troubles their conquerors. 2d, The class of Republicans led by Seward, offering to surrender any thing to save the Union. (Applause.) Their gospel is the Constitution (applause), and the slave clause is their sermon on the mount. (Laughter and applause.) They think that at the judgment-day, the blacker the sins they have committed to save the Union, the clearer will be their title to heaven. 3d, The rest of the Republicans, led by the *Tribune*, — all honor to the *Tribune*, faithful and true! — who consider their honor pledged to fulfil in office the promises made in the canvass. Their motto is: "The Chicago platform, every inch of it; not a hair's-breadth of the territories shall be surrendered to slavery." (Applause.) But they, too, claim the cannon's mouth to protect forts, defend the flag, and save the Union. At the head of this section, we have every reason to believe, stands MR. ABRAHAM LINCOLN.

All these are the actors on the stage. But the foundation on which all stand divides only into two parts: those who like slavery and mean it shall last — those who hate it and mean it shall die. In the boiling gulf goes on the perpetual conflict of acid and alkali; all these classes are but bubbles on the surface. The upper millstone is *right*, and the lower *wrong*. Between them, governments and parliaments, parties and compromises, are being slowly ground to powder.

Broadly stated, the South plans a Southern Confederacy to uphold slavery — the North clings to the Union to uphold trade and secure growth. Without the Union, Mr. Seward tells us we can neither be safe, rich, strong, nor happy. We used to think justice was before thrift, and nobleness better than happiness. I place no great reliance on that prudent patriotism which is the child of interest. The *Tribune*, unusually frank, pre-eminently honorable and lofty as has been its tone of late, still says, "Be it the business of the people everywhere to forget the negro, and remember only the country." (Applause.)

After drifting, a dreary night of thirty years, before the hurricane, our ship of State is going to pieces on the lee shore of slavery. Every one confesses that the poison of our body politic is slavery. European critics, in view of it, have pronounced the existence of the Union hitherto a "fortunate accident." Orators floated into fame on one inspired phrase, "irrepressible conflict." Jefferson died foreseeing that this was the rock on which we should split. Even Mr. Webster, speaking with bated breath, in the cold chill of 1850, still dared to be a statesman, and offered to meet the South on this question, suggesting a broad plan for the cure of our dread disease. But now, with the Union dropping asunder, with every brain and tongue active, we have yet to hear the first statesman word, the first proposal to consider the fountain and origin of all our ills. We look in vain through Mr. Seward's speech for one hint or suggestion as to any method of dealing with our terrible hurt. Indeed,

1*

one of his terrors of disunion is, that it will give room for
"an European, an uncompromising hostility to slavery."
Such an hostility — the irrepressible conflict of right and
wrong — William H. Seward, in 1861, pronounces "fearful"!
To describe the great conflict of the age, the first of American statesmen, in the year of Garibaldi and Italy, can find
no epithet but "fearful."

The servile silence of the 7th of March, 1850, is outdone,
and, to New York, Massachusetts yields the post of infamy
which her great Senator has hitherto filled.   Yes, of all the
doctors bending over the patient, not one dares to name his
disease, except the *Tribune*, which advises him to forget it!
Throughout half of the great cities of the North, every one
who touches on it is mobbed into silence!   This is, indeed,
the saddest feature of our times.

Let us, then, who, unlike Mr. Seward, are not afraid to
tell, even now, all and just what we wish — let us look at
the real nature of the crisis in which we stand.   The *Tribune* says we should "forget the negro."   It seems to me
that all our past, all our present, and all our future com-
mand us at this moment to think of nothing but the negro.
(Slight laughter derisively.)

Let me tell you why.   Mr. Seward says, "The first object
of every human society is safety;" I think the first duty of
society is JUSTICE.   Alexander Hamilton said, "Justice is
the end of government.   It is the end of civil society."   If
any other basis of safety or gain were honest, it would be
impossible.   "A prosperous iniquity," says Jeremy Taylor,
"is the most unprofitable condition in the world."   The nation which, in moments when great moral questions disturb
its peace, consults first for its own *safety*, is atheist and cow-
ard, and there are three chances out of four that it will end
by being knave.   We were not sent into the world to plant
cities, to make Unions or save them.   Seeing that all men
are born equal, our first civil duty is to see that our laws
treat them so.   The convulsion of this hour is the effort of
the nation to do this, its duty, while politicians and parties
strive to balk it of its purpose.   The nation agonizes this
hour to recognize man as man, forgetting the color, condition, sex, and creed.

Our Revolution earned us only *independence*.   Whatever
our fathers meant, the chief lesson of that hour was that

America belongs to Americans. That generation learned it thoroughly; the second inherited it as a prejudice; we, the third, have our bones and blood made of it. When thought passes through purpose into character, it becomes the unchangeable basis of national life. That Revolutionary lesson need never be learned again, and will never die out. Let a British fleet, with admirals of the blue and red, cover our Atlantic coast, and in ten days, Massachusetts and Carolina will stand shoulder to shoulder, the only rivalry, who shall die nearest the foe. (Loud applause, with cries of "Good.")

That principle is all our Revolution directly taught us. Massachusetts was hide-bound in the aristocracy of classes for year after. The bar and the orthodox pulpit were our House of Lords. A Baptist clergyman was little better than a negro. The five points of Massachusetts decency were, to trace your lineage to the Mayflower, graduate at Harvard College, be a good lawyer or a member of an orthodox church, — either would answer (laughter), — pay your debts, and frighten your child to sleep by saying "Thomas Jefferson." Our theological aristocracy went down before the stalwart blows of Baptist, Unitarian, and Freethinker — before Channing and Abner Kneeland. Virginia slaveholders, making theoretical democracy their passion, conquered the Federal Government, and emancipated the working classes of New England. Bitter was the cup to honest Federalism and the Essex junto. To-day, Massachusetts only holds to the lips of Carolina a beaker of the same beverage. I know no man who has analyzed this passage in our history so well as Richard Hildreth. The last thirty years have been the flowering out of this lesson. The Democratic principle, crumbling classes into men, has been working down from pulpits and judges' seats, through shop-boards and shoe-benches, to Irish hodmen, and reached the negro at last. The long toil of a century cries out "*Eureka!*" — I have found it! — the diamond of an immortal soul and an equal manhood under a black skin as truly as under a white one. For this, Leggett labored and Lovejoy died. For this, the bravest soul of the century went up to God from a Virginia scaffold. (Hisses and applause.) For this, young men gave up their May of youth, and old men the honors and ease of age. It went through the land writing history afresh, setting up and pulling down parties, riving sects, mowing down colossal reputations, making us veil our faces in shame at the baseness of our youth's idols, sending bankrupt statesmen to dishonored graves.

We stand to-day just as Hancock and Adams and Jefferson stood, when stamp act and tea tax, Patrick Henry's eloquence and the massacre of March 5th. Otis' blood and Bunker Hill, had borne them to July, 1776. Suppose at that moment John Adams had cried out, "Now let the people everywhere forget Independence, and remember only 'God save the King'!" (Laughter.) The toil of a whole generation — thirty years — has been spent in examining this question of the rights and place of the negro; the whole earnest thought of the nation given to it; old parties have been worked against it, new ones grown out of it; it stifles all other questions; the great interests of the nation necessarily suffer, men refusing to think of any thing but this; it struggles up through all compromises, asserting its right to be heard; no green withes of eloquence or cunning, trade, pulpit, Congress, or college, succeed in binding this Samson; the business of the seaboard begs it may be settled, no matter how; the whole South is determined to have it met, proclaiming that it does not secede because of Personal Liberty Laws or a Republican President, but because of the state of *Northern feeling* of which these are *signs.* It is not Northern laws or officers they fear, but Northern *conscience.* Why, then, should not the North accept the issue, and try to settle the question forever? You may run the Missouri line to the Pacific, but Garrison still lives; and while he does, South Carolina hates and fears Massachusetts. (Applause.) No congressional resolves can still our brains or stifle our hearts; till you do, the slaveholder feels that New England is his natural foe. There can therefore be no real peace till we settle the slave question. If thirty years of debate have not fitted us to meet it, when shall we be able?

But the most honest Republicans say a State has no right to secede; we will show first that we have a government, and then, not before, settle disputed questions. Suppose a State has no right to secede, of what consequence is that? A Union is made up of willing States, not of conquered provinces. There are some rights, quite perfect, yet wholly incapable of being enforced. A husband or wife who can only keep the other partner within the bond by locking the doors and standing armed before them, had better submit to peaceable separation. (Applause.) A firm where one partner refuses to act, has a full right to his services, but how compel them? South Carolina may be punished for her fault in going out of the Union, but that does not keep her in it. Why not recognize soberly the nature and necessity of our position? Why not, like statesmen, remember that homogeneous nations, like France, tend to centralization; confederacies, like ours, tend inevitably to dismemberment? France is the slow, still deposit of ages on central granite; only the globe's convulsion can rive it! We are the rich mud of the Mississippi; every flood shifts it from one side to the other of the channel. Nations, like Austria, victim States, held under the lock and key of despotism, — or like ourselves, a herd of States, hunting for their food together, — must expect that any quarrel may lead to disunion. Beside, *Inter arma, silent leges* — Armies care nothing for constables. This is not a case at law, but revolution.

Let us not, however, too anxiously grieve over the Union of 1787. Real Unions are not made, they grow. This was made, like an artificial waterfall or a Connecticut nutmeg. It was not an oak which to-day a tempest shatters. It was a wall hastily built, in hard times, of round boulders; the cement has crumbled, and the smooth stones, obeying the law of gravity, tumble here and there. Why should we seek to stop them, merely to show that we have a right and can? That were only a waste of means and temper. Let us build, like the pyramids, a fabric which every natural law guarantees; or, better still, *plant* a Union whose life survives the ages, and quietly gives birth to its successor.

Mr. Seward's last speech, which he confesses does not express his real convictions, denies every principle, but one, that he proclaimed in his campaign addresses; that one — which, at Lansing, he expressly said "he was ashamed to confess" — that one is this: Every thing is to be sacrificed to save the Union. I am not aware that, on any public occasion, varied and wide as have been his discussions and topics, he has ever named the truth or the virtue which he would not sacrifice to save the Union. For thirty years, there has been stormy and searching discussion of profound moral questions; one, whom his friends call our only statesman, has spoken often on all; yet he has never named the sin which he does not think its saving of the Union would not change into a virtue.

Remembering this element of his statesmanship, let us listen to the key-note of his late speech: "The first object of every human society is safety or security, for which, if need be, they will and they must sacrifice every other."

I will not stop to say that, even with his explanation, his principle is equivocal, and, if unlimited, false; that, unqualified, it justifies every crime, and would have prevented every glory of history; that by it, James II. and Bonaparte were saints; under one sense, the Pilgrims were madmen, and under another, the Puritans did right to hang Quakers. But grant it. Suppose the Union means wealth, culture, happiness, and safety, man has no right to buy either by crime.

Many years ago, on the floor of Congress, Kentucky and Tennessee both confessed that "the dissolution of the Union was the dissolution of slavery." Last month, Senator Johnson of Tennessee said, "If I were an abolitionist, and wanted to accomplish the abolition of slavery in the Southern States, the first step I would take would be to break the bonds of this Union. I believe the continuance of slavery depends on the preservation of this Union, and a compliance with all the guarantees of the Constitution." In September last (at La-Crosse) Mr. Seward himself said, "What are they [the Southern States] in for, but to have slavery saved for them by the Federal Union? Why would they go out, for they could not maintain and defend themselves against their own slaves?" In this last speech, he tells us it is the Union which restricts the opposition to slavery within narrow limits, and prevents it from being, like that of Europe, a "direct and uncompromising" demand for abolition.

Now, if the Union created for us a fresh Golconda every month, if it made every citizen wise as Solomon, blameless as St. John, and safe as an angel in the courts of Heaven, to cling to it would still be a damnable crime, hateful to God, while its cement was the blood of the negro — while it, and it alone, made the crime of slaveholding possible in fifteen States.

Mr. Seward is a power in the State. It is worth while to understand his course. It cannot be caprice. His position decides that of millions. The instinct that leads him to take it shows his guess (and he rarely errs) what the majority intend. I reconcile thus the utter difference and opposition of his campaign speeches, and his last one. I think he went West, sore at the loss of the nomination, but with too much good sense, perhaps magnanimity, to act over again Webster's sullen part when Taylor stole his rights.

Still, Mr. Seward, though philosophic, though keen to analyze and unfold the theory of our politics, is not cunning in plans. He is only the hand and tongue; his brain lives in private life on the Hudson River side. Acting under that guidance, he thought Mr. Lincoln not likely to go beyond, even if he were able to keep, the whole Chicago platform. Accordingly, he said, "I will give free rein to my natural feelings and real convictions, till these Abolitionists of the Republican ranks shall cry, 'Oh, what a mistake! We ought to have nominated Seward; another time we will not be balked.'" Hence the hot eloquence and fearless tone of those prairie speeches. He returns to Washington, finds Mr. Lincoln sturdily insisting that his honor is pledged to keep, in office, every promise made in the platform. Then Mr. Seward shifts his course, saying, "Since my abolitionism cannot take the wind from my rival's sails, I'll get credit as a Conservative. Accepting the premiership, I will forestall public opinion, and do all possible to bind the coming administration to a policy which I originate." He offers to postpone the whole Chicago Platform, in order to save the Union — though last October, at Chicago, he told us postponement never settles any thing, whether it is a lawsuit or national question; better be beat and try again, than postpone.

This speech of Mr. Seward I regard as a declaration of war against the avowed policy of the incoming President. If Lincoln were an Andrew Jackson, as his friends aver, he would dismiss Mr. Seward from his Cabinet. The incoming administration, if honest and firm, has two enemies to fight, Mr. Seward and the South.

His power is large. Already he has swept our Adams

into the vortex, making him offer to sacrifice the whole Republican platform, though, as events have turned, he has sacrificed only his own personal honor. Fifteen years ago, John Quincy Adams prophesied that the Union would not last twenty years. He little thought that disunion, when it came, would swallow his son's honor in its gulf.*

At such hours, New England Senators and Representatives have, from the very idea of their ultraism, little or no direct weight in Congress. But while New England is the brain of the Union, and therefore foreshadows what will be public opinion in the plastic West five years hence, it is of momentous consequence that the people here should make their real feelings known; that the pulpit and press should sound the bugle-note of utter defiance to slavery itself — Union or no Union, Constitution or no Constitution, freedom for every man between the oceans, and from the hot Gulf to the frozen Pole! You may as well dam up Niagara with bulrushes as bind our anti-slavery purpose with congressional compromise. The South knows it. While she holds out her hand for Seward's offer, she keeps her eye fixed on us, to see what we think. Let her see that we laugh it to scorn. Sacrifice any thing to keep the slaveholding States in the Union? God forbid! we will rather build a bridge of gold, and pay their toll over it — accompany them out with glad noise of trumpets, and " speed the parting guest." Let them not "stand on the order of their going, but go at once"! Let them take the forts, empty our arsenals and sub-treasuries, and we will lend them beside jewels of gold and jewels of silver, and Egypt be glad when they are departed. (Laughter and applause.)

But let the world distinctly understand why they go — to save slavery; and why we rejoice in their departure — because we know their declaration of independence is the jubilee of the slave. The eyes of the world are fixed on us as the great example of self-government. When this Union goes to pieces, it is a shock to the hopes of the struggling millions of Europe. All lies bear bitter fruit. To-day is the inevitable fruit of our fathers' faithless compromise in 1787. For the sake of the future, in freedom's name, let

---

* Since this was said, Mr. Adams has had his reward — winning high office by treachery to his party, as his father did before, and as his grandfather tried to do and failed.

thinking Europe understand clearly why we sever. They saw Mr. Seward paint, at Chicago, our utter demoralization, Church and State, government and people, all classes, educated and uneducated — all brought by the Slave Power, he said, to think slavery a blessing, and do any thing to save it. So utter did he consider this demoralization, that he despaired of Native Americans, and trusted to the hunted patriots and the refuse of Europe, which the emigrant trains bore by his house, for the salvation of the valley of the Mississippi. To-day, they see that very man kneeling to that Slave Power, and begging her to take all, but only consent to grant him such a Union — Union with such a Power! How, then, shall Kossuth answer, when Austria laughs him to scorn? Shall Europe see the slaveholder kick the reluctant and kneeling North out of such a Union? How, then, shall Garibaldi dare look in the face of Napoleon? If, therefore, it were only to honor self-government, to prove that it educates men, not pedlers and cowards, let us proclaim our faith that honest labor can stand alone; its own right hand amply able to earn its bread and defend its rights (applause); and, if it were not so, our readiness at any cost, to welcome disunion, when it comes bringing freedom to four million of hapless slaves! (Applause.) What a sad comment on free institutions, that they have produced a South of tyrants, and a North of cowards; a South, ready to face any peril to save slavery, and a North unwilling to risk a dollar to serve freedom?

Why do I set so little value on the Union? Because I consider it a failure; certainly, so far as slavery is concerned, it is a failure. If you doubt me, look at the picture of its effects which Mr. Seward painted at Chicago.

Look at our history. Under it, 700,000 slaves have increased to 4,000,000. We have paid $800,000,000 directly to the support of slavery. This secession will cost the Union and business $200,000,000 more. The loss which this disturbing force has brought to our trade and industry, within sixty years, it would be safe to call $500,000,000. Is the Union a pecuniary success? Under it, slavery has been strong enough to rule the nation for sixty years, and now breaks it to pieces because it can rule no longer. Under it, public morals have been so lowered, that while, at its outset, nine men out of ten were proud to be called Abo-

2

litionists, now, nine out of ten would deem it not only an insult, but a pecuniary injury, to be charged with being so. Ever since it existed, its friends have confessed that to save it, it was necessary and proper to crush free speech. Witness John Adams' sedition laws. Witness mobs of well-dressed merchants in every Northern city now. Witness one-half of the Republican party lamenting free speech, this hour, throughout the North.

Mr. Seward confessed, at Chicago, that neither free speech nor free suffrage existed in one-half of the States. No Northern man can trade, live, or talk there. For twenty years, men have been mobbed, robbed, lynched, hung, and burned there, solely for loving liberty; and while the Federal Government never lifted a finger to prevent or punish it, the very States whose citizens have been outraged, have been too indifferent even to remonstrate. Massachusetts, who once remonstrated, saw her own agent mobbed out of Charleston with her full consent.

Before the Union existed, Washington and Jefferson uttered the boldest anti-slavery opinions; to-day they would be lynched in their own homes; and their sentiments have been mobbed this very year in every great city of the North. The Fugitive Slave Bill could never have been passed nor executed in the days of Jay. Now, no man who hopes for office dares to insist that it is unconstitutional. Slavery has turned our churches of Christ to churches of commerce.

John Quincy Adams, the child of our earlier civilization, said the Union was worthless, weighed against that liberty it was meant to secure. Mr. Seward, child of the Union, says there are few men, and there ought to be few, who would not prefer saving the Union to securing freedom; and standing to-day at the head of nineteen million of free men, he confesses he does not deem it prudent to express his "most cherished convictions" on this subject,* while

---

* Mr. Seward said, at St. Paul, last September: "I do not believe there has been one day, since 1787, until now, when slavery had any power in this government, except what it derived from buying up men of weak virtue, no principle, and great cupidity, and terrifying men of weak nerve in the Free States." * * * "Fellow-citizens, either in one way or the other, whether you agree with me in attributing it to the interposition of Divine Providence or not, this battle has been fought, this victory has been won. Slavery to-day is, for the first time, not only powerless, but without influence in the American

every honest man fears, and three-fourths of Mr. Seward's
followers hope, that the North, in this conflict of right and
wrong, will, spite of Horace Greeley's warning, "love Liberty less than Profit, dethrone Conscience, and set up Commerce in its stead." You know it. A Union whose despotism is so cruel and searching that one-half our lawyers
and one-half our merchants stifle conscience for bread — in
the name of Martin Luther and John Milton, of Algernon
Sydney and Henry Vane, of John Jay and Samuel Adams,
I declare such a Union a failure.

It is for the chance of saving such a Union that Mr.
Seward and Mr. Adams break in Washington all the promises of the canvass, and countenance measures which stifle
the conscience and confuse the moral sense of the North.
Say not that my criticism of them is harsh. I know their
philosophy. It is, conciliate, compromise, postpone, practise
finesse, make promises, or break them, do any thing, to gain
time and concentrate the North against slavery. Our fathers
tried that policy in 1787. That they miserably failed is
proved by a Capitol filled with knaves and traitors, yet able
to awe and ruin honest men. It was tried in 1821, and
failed. It was tried in 1850, and failed. Who is auda-
cious enough to ask another trial? The Republicans say,
"Conciliate, use soft language, organize — behind the door —
bands of volunteers; and when we have saved Washington,
we may dare speak out." That is good policy for midnight
conspirators. But if we are a government, if we are a nation, we should say, "Tell the truth! If coercion is our
policy, tell the truth. Call for volunteers in every State,
and vindicate the honor of the nation in the light of the
sun!" (Applause.)

The cunning which equivocates to-day, in order to secure
a peaceful inauguration on the 4th of March, will yield up

Republic." * * * "For the first time in the history of the Republic, the Slave Power has not even the power to terrify or alarm
the freeman so as to make him submit and scheme and coincide and
compromise. It rails now with a feeble voice, as it thundered in our
ears for twenty or thirty years past. With a feeble and muttering
voice, they cry out that they will tear the Union to pieces. Who's
afraid? They complain that if we will not surrender our principles
and our system and our right — being a majority — to rule, and if
we will not accept their system, and such rules as they will give us,
they will go out of the Union. Who's afraid? Nobody's afraid;
nobody can be bought." [Yet now Mr. Seward himself trembles!]

all its principles before the 1st of July.   Beside, when
opiate speeches have dulled the Northern conscience, and
kneeling speeches have let down its courage, who can be
sure that even Seward's voice, if he retain the wish, can
conjure up again such a North as stands face to face wi h
Southern arrogance to-day?

The Union, then, is a failure.   What harm can come
from disunion, and what good?

The seceding States will form a Southern Confederacy.
We may judge of its future from the history of Mexico.
The Gulf States intend to re-open the slave trade.   If
Kentucky and Tennessee, Virginia, Maryland, and North
Carolina secede, the opening of that trade will ruin them,
and they will gravitate to us, free.   Louisiana cannot secede, except on paper; the omnipotent West needs her territory as the mouth of its river.   She must stay with us as
a State or a conquered province, and may have her choice.
(Laughter.)   Beside, she stands on sugar, and free trade
bankrupts her.   Consider the rest of the Slave States as
one Power, how can it harm us?   Let us see the ground
of Mr. Seward's fears.   Will it increase our expenses or
lessen our receipts?   No; every one of those States costs
the Union more than it contributes to it.   Can it harm us
by attacks?   States without commerce or manufactures, and
with an army of four millions of natural enemies encamped
among them, have given bonds to keep the peace.   Will
they leave us so small and weak by going that we cannot
stand alone?   Let us see.   There is no reason to suppose
that the Free States, except California, will not cling together.
Idem velle, idem nolle — to like and dislike the same things,
says the Latin proverb, is friendship.   When a great number of persons agree in a great number of things, that en-
sures a union; that is not the case with the North and
South, therefore we separate; that is the case with the
whole North, therefore we shall remain united.   How
strong shall we be?   Our territory will be twice as large
as Austria, three times as large as France, four times as
large as Spain, six times as large as Italy, seven times as
large as Great Britain.   Those nations have proved, for a
considerable period, that they had sufficient land to stand
on.   Our population will be about nineteen millions — more
than the Union had in 1840.   I do not think we were much

afraid of anybody in 1840. Our blood is largely Yankee, a race that saved Carolina from her own Tories, in the Revolution. (Laughter.) Without that hindrance, we could fight now, certainly, as well as we did then; and then, with three million men only, we measured swords with the ablest nation of Europe, and conquered. I think, therefore, we have no reason to be very nervously anxious now. Indeed, Mr. Seward's picture of the desolation and military weakness of the divided States, if intended for the North, is the emptiest lie in his speech. I said *lie;* I meant it. I will tell you why. Because one William H. Seward said, last fall, at Lansing, "We are maintaining a standing army at the heavy cost of one thousand dollars per man, and a standing navy — for what? to protect Michigan or Massachusetts, New York or Ohio? *No; there is not a nation on the face of the earth which would dare to attack these Free States, or any of them, if they were even disunited.* We are doing it in order that slaves may not escape from Slave States into the Free, and to secure those States from domestic insurrection; and because, if we provoke a foreign foe, slavery cries out that it is in danger." Surely, the speaker of those words has no right to deny that our expenses and danger will be less, and our power to meet both greater, when the Slave States are gone.

Indeed, everybody knows this. And this trembling dread of losing the Union, which so frightens the people that, in view of it, Mr. Seward, as a practical man, dares not now tell, as he says, what he really thinks and wishes, is the child of his and Webster's insincere idolatry of the Union. To serve party and personal ambition, they made a god of the Union; and to-day their invention returns to plague the inventors. They made the people slaves to a falsehood; and that same deluded people have turned their fetters into gags for Mr. Seward's lips. Thank God for the retribution!

But the Union created commerce; disunion will kill it. The Union the mother of commerce? I doubt it. I question whether the genius and energy of the Yankee race are not the parent of commerce and the fountain of wealth, much more than the Union. That race, in Holland, first created a country, and then, standing on piles, called modern commerce into being. That race, in England, with territory

2*

just wide enough to keep its eastern and western harbors apart, monopolized, for centuries, the trade of the world, and annexed continents only as coffers wherein to garner its wealth. Who shall say that the same blood, with only New England for its anchorage, could not drag the wealth of the West into its harbors? Who shall say that the fertile lands of Virginia and the Mississippi enrich us because they will to do so, and not because they are compelled? As long as New England is made of granite and the nerves of her sons of steel, she will be, as she always has been, the brain of North America, united or disunited ; and harnessing the elements, steam and lightning, to her car of conquest, she will double the worth of every prairie acre by her skill, cover ocean with her canvas, and gather the wealth of the western hemisphere into her harbors.

Despite, then, of Seward's foreboding, our confederacy will be strong, safe, and rich. Honest it will be, and therefore happy. Its nobleness will be, that, laughing at prophets, and scorning chances, it has taken the prop from the slave system, and in one night the whole fabric will tumble to pieces. Disunion is abolition! That is all the value disunion has for me. I care little for forms of government, or extent of territory ; whether ten States or thirty make up the Union. No foreign State dare touch us, united or disunited. It matters not to me whether Massachusetts is worth one thousand millions, as now, or two thousand millions, as she might be, if she had no Carolina to feed, protect, and carry the mails for. The music of disunion to me is, that at its touch, the slave breaks into voice, shouting his jubilee.

What supports slavery? Northern bayonets, calming the masters' fears. Mr. Seward's words, which I have just quoted, tell you what he thinks the sole use of our army and navy. Disunion leaves God's natural laws to work their good results. God gives every animal means of self-protection. Under God's law, insurrection is the tyrant's check. Let us stand out of the path, and allow the divine law to have free course.

Next, Northern opinion is the opiate of Southern conscience. Disunion changes that. Public opinion forms governments, and again governments react to mould opin-

ion. Here is a government just as much permeated by
slavery as China or Japan is with idolatry.

The Republican party take possession of this government. How are they to undermine the Slave Power?
That power is composed, 1st, of the inevitable influence of
wealth, $2,000,000,000, — the worth of the slaves in the
Union, — so much capital drawing to it the sympathy of all
other capital ; 2d, of the artificial aristocracy created by the
three-fifths slave basis of the Constitution ; 3d, by the potent and baleful prejudice of color.

The aristocracy of the Constitution! Where have you
seen an aristocracy with half its power? You may take a
small town here in New England, with a busy, active population of 2,500, and three or four such men as Gov. Aiken,
of South Carolina, riding leisurely to the polls, and throw-
ing their visiting cards in for ballots, will blot out the entire
influence of that New England town in the Federal Government. That is your Republicanism! Then, when you add
to that the element of prejudice, which is concentrated in
the epithet that spells negro with two "gg's," you make the
three-strand cable of the Slave Power — the prejudice of
race, the omnipotence of money, and the almost irresistible
power of aristocracy. That is the Slave Power.

How is Mr. Lincoln to undermine it while in the Union?
Certainly, by turning every atom of patronage and pecuniary profit in the keeping of the Federal Government to the
support of freedom. You know that policy has been always
acted upon ever since Washington, and it has been openly
avowed ever since Fillmore. No man was to receive any
office who was not sound on the slavery question. You remember the debate in the Senate, when that was distinctly
avowed to be the policy of Mr. Fillmore. You remember
Mr. Clay letting it drop out accidentally, in debate, that the
slaveholders had always closely watched the Cabinet, and
kept a majority there, in order to preserve the ascendency
of slavery. This is the policy which, in the course of fifty
years, has built up the Slave Power. Now, how is the Republican party ever to beat that Power down? By revers-
ing that policy, in favor of freedom. Cassius Clay said to
me, five years ago: "If you will allow me to have the patronage of this government five years, and exercise it re-
morselessly, down to New Orleans; never permit any one

but an avowed Abolitionist to hold office under the Federal
Government, I will revolutionize the Slave States themselves in two administrations." That is a scheme of efficient
politics. But the Republican party has never yet professed
any such policy.

Mr. Greeley, on the contrary, avowed in the *Tribune*,
that he had often voted for a slaveholder willingly, and he
never expected the time would come when he should lay
down the principle of refusing to vote for a slaveholder to
office; and that sentiment has not only been reiterated by
others of the Republican party, but has never been disa-
vowed by any one. But suppose you could develop politics
up to this idea, that the whole patronage of the government
should be turned in favor of Abolition; it would take two
or three generations to overthrow what the Slave Power
has done in sixty years, with the strength of aristocracy and
the strength of prejudice on its side. With only the patronage of the government in its control, the Republican
party must work slowly to regenerate the government
against those two elements in opposition, when, with them
in its favor, the Slave Power has been some sixty years in
bringing about such a result as we see around us. To re-
verse this, and work only with the patronage of the government, it would take you long to effect the cure. In my soul,
I believe that a dissolution of the Union, sure to result
speedily in the abolition of slavery, would be a lesser evil
than the slow, faltering, diseased, gradual dying-out of
slavery, constantly poisoning us with the festering remains
of this corrupt political, social, and literary state. I believe
a sudden, conclusive, definite disunion, resulting in the abolition of slavery, in the disruption of the Northern mind
from all connection with it, all vassalage to it, *immediately*,
would be a better, healthier, and more wholesome cure, than
to let the Republican party exert this gradual influence
through the power of the government for thirty or sixty
years.

We are seeking the best way to get rid of a great national
evil Mr. Seward's way is to put down the Union as a
"fixed fact," and then educate politics up to a certain level.
In that way we have to live, like Sinbad, with Cushing, and
Hillard, and Hallett, and O'Connor, and Douglas, and men
like them, on our shoulders, for the next thirty or forty

years; with the Deweys and President Lords, and all that
class of men, — and all this timid servility of the press, all
this lack of virtue and manhood, all this corruption of the
pulpit, all this fossil hunkerism, all this selling of the soul
for a mess of pottage, is to linger, working in the body politic for thirty or forty years, and we are gradually to eliminate the disease! What an awful future! What a miser-
able chronic disease! What a wreck of a noble nation the
American Republic is to be for fifty years!

And why? Only to save a piece of parchment that El-
bridge Gerry had instinct enough to think did not deserve
saving, as long ago as 1789! Mr. Seward would leave
New York united to New Orleans, with the hope (sure to be
balked) of getting freer and freer from year to year. I want
to place her, at once, in the same relation towards New Orleans that she bears to Liverpool. You can do it, the moment you break the political tie. What will that do? I
will tell you. The New York pulpit is to-day one end of a
magnetic telegraph, of which the New Orleans cotton market
is the other. The New York stock-market is one end of
the magnetic telegraph, and the *Charleston Mercury* is the
other. New York statesmanship! Why, even in the lips
of Seward, it is sealed, or half sealed, by considerations that
take their rise in the cane-brakes and cotton-fields of fifteen
States. Break up this Union, and the ideas of South Carolina will have no more influence on Seward than those of
Palmerston. The wishes of New Orleans would have no
more influence on Chief Justice Bigelow than the wishes of
London. The threats of Davis, Toombs, and Keitt will
have no more influence on the *Tribune* than the thunders
of the London *Times* or the hopes of the Chartists. Our
Bancrofts will no longer write history with one eye fixed on
Democratic success, nor our Websters invent "laws of God"
to please Mr. Senator Douglas. We shall have as close
connection, as much commerce; we shall still have a common language, a common faith and common race, the same
common social life; we shall intermarry just the same; we
shall have steamers running just as often and just as rapidly
as now. But what cares Dr. Dewey for the opinion of Liverpool? Nothing! What cares he for the opinion of Washington? Every thing! Break the link, and New York
springs up like the fountain relieved from a mountain load,

and assumes her place among decent cities. I mean no
special praise of the English courts, pulpit, or press, by these
comparisons; my only wish is to show that however close
the commercial relations might continue to be between
North and South, and in spite of that common faith and
common tongue and common history, which would continue
to hold these thirty States together, still, as in the case of
this country and England, wedded still by those ties, the
mere sundering of a political union would leave each half
free, as that of 1776 did, from a very large share of the
corrupt influence of the other.

That is what I mean by Disunion. I mean to take Massachusetts, and leave her exactly as she is, commercially.
She shall manufacture for the South just as Lancashire does.
I know what an influence the South has on the manufac-
turers and clergy of England; — that is inevitable, in the
nature of things. We have only human nature to work
with, and we cannot raise it up to the level of angels. We
shall never get beyond the sphere of human selfishness, but
we can lift this human nature up to a higher level, if we can
but remove the weight of this political relation which now
rests upon it. What I would do with Massachusetts is this
— I would make her, in relation to South Carolina, just
what England is. I would that I could float her off, and
anchor her in mid-ocean!

Severed from us, South Carolina must have a government. You see now a reign of terror — threats to raise
means. That can only last a day. Some system must give
support to a government. It is an expensive luxury. You
must lay taxes to support it. Where will you levy your
taxes? They must rest on productions. Productions are
the result of skilled labor. You must educate your laborer,
if you would have the means for carrying on a government.
Despotisms are cheap; free governments are a dear luxury
— the machinery is complicated and expensive. If the
South wants a theoretical republic, she must pay for it —
she must have a basis for taxation. How will she pay for
it? Why, Massachusetts, with a million workmen — men,
women, and children, — the little feet that can just toddle
bringing chips from the wood-pile, — Massachusetts only
pays her own board and lodging, and lays by about four per
cent a year. And South Carolina, with one-half idlers,

and the other half slaves,—a slave doing only half the work of a free man,—only one-quarter of the population actually at work, how much do you suppose she lays up? Lays up a loss! By all the laws of political economy, she lays up bankruptcy; of course she does! Put her out, and let her see how sheltered she has been from the laws of trade by the Union! The free labor of the North pays her plantation patrol; we pay for her government, we pay for her postage, and for every thing else. Launch her out, and let her see if she can make the year's ends meet! And when she tries, she must educate her labor in order to get the basis for taxation. Educate slaves! Make a locomotive with its furnaces of open wire work, fill them with anthracite coal, and when you have raised it to white heat, mount and drive it through a powder magazine, and you are safe, compared with a slaveholding community educating its slaves. But South Carolina must do it, in order to get the basis for taxation to support an independent government. The moment she does it, she removes the safeguard of slavery. What is the contest in Virginia now? Between the men who want to make their slaves mechanics, for the increased wages it will secure, and the men who oppose, for fear of the influence it will have on the general security of slave property and white throats. Just that dispute will go on, wherever the Union is dissolved. Slavery comes to an end by the laws of trade. Hang up your Sharp's rifle, my valorous friend! The slave does not ask the help of your musket. He only says, like old Diogenes to Alexander, "Stand out of my light!" Just take your awkward proportions, you Yankee Democrat and Republican, out of the light and heat of God's laws of political economy, and they will melt the slave's chains away!

Indeed, I much doubt whether the South can maintain her cotton culture at all, as a separate, Slaveholding Government. Cotton is only an annual in the United States. In St. Domingo and the tropics it is a tree lasting from five to twenty years. Within the Union, it is then, strictly speaking, a forced product: or, at least, it touches the highest northern belt of possible culture, only possible there under very favorable circumstances. We all know how hard and keen is the competition of this generation; men clutching bread only by restless hands and brains. Expose

now our cotton to the full competition of India, Africa, and
the tropics ; burden it by taxes, with the full cost of a Slaveholding Government, necessarily an expensive one, — a tax
it has never yet felt, having shirked it on to the North ; —
quicken other cotton fields into greater activity by the un-
willingness of France and England to trust their supply to
States convulsed by political quarrels, — and then see if, in
such circumstances, the price of cotton in the markets of
the world will not rule so low, that to raise it by slovenly
slave-culture will not be utter loss — so utter as to drive it
wholly from our States, at least while they remain Slave
States.

Indeed, the Gulf States are essentially in a feudal condition, an aristocracy resting on slaves, — no middle class.
To sustain Government on the costly model of our age ne-
cessitates a middle class of trading, manufacturing energy.
The merchant of the nineteenth century spurns to be a
subordinate. The introduction of such a class will create
in the Gulf States that very irrepressible conflict which
they leave us to avoid — which, alive now in the Border
States, makes these unwilling to secede, — which once created will soon undermine the aristocracy of the Gulf States
and bring them back to us free.

Take your distorted Union, your nightmare monster, out
of the light and range of those laws of trade and competition ; then, without any sacrifice on your part, slavery will
go to pieces God made it a law of his universe, that vil-
lany should always be loss ; and if you will only not attempt,
with your puny efforts, to stand betwixt the inevitable laws
of God's kingdom, as you are doing to-day, and have done
for sixty years, by the vigor that the industry of sixteen
States has been able to infuse into the sluggish veins of the
South, slavery will drop to pieces by the very influence of
the competition of the nineteenth century. That is what
we mean by Disunion !

That is my *coercion!* Northern pulpits cannonading the
Southern conscience ; Northern competition emptying its
pockets ; educated slaves awaking its fears ; civilization
and Christianity beckoning the South into their sisterhood.
Soon every breeze that sweeps over Carolina will bring to
our ears the music of repentance, and even she will carve

on her Palmetto, " We hold this truth to be self-evident —
that all men are created equal."

All hail, then, Disunion! · " Beautiful on the mountains
are the feet of him that bringeth good tidings, that publish-
eth peace, that saith unto Zion, Thy God reigneth."   The
sods of Bunker Hill shall be greener, now that their great
purpose is accomplished.   Sleep in peace, martyr of Har-
per's Ferry! — your life was not given in vain.   Rejoice,
spirits of Fayette and Kosciusko! — the only stain upon
your swords is passing away.   Soon, throughout all America, there shall be neither power nor wish to hold a slave.

3

PROGRESS.

In accordance with his regular engagement, WENDELL
PHILLIPS, Esq., addressed the Twenty-eighth Congrega-
tional Society in Music Hall, Sunday forenoon, 17th inst.
There were four thousand persons present, many unable to
find seats. Mr. Phillips spoke upon " Progress," from the
following text : —

"And Jacob said unto Pharaoh, The days of the years of my pilgrimage are an hundred and thirty years : few and evil have the days
of the years of my life been, and have not attained unto the days of
the years of the life of my fathers in the days of their pilgrimage."

Thus spoke a prince who had won from his elder brother
both birthright and blessing; who had seen "the angels of
God ascending and descending;" was able to say, " With
my staff I passed over this Jordan, and now I am become
two bands;" who had seen God face to face, and still lived;
to whom was pledged the Divine promise, " I will make of
thee a great nation; in thy seed shall all the families of the
earth be blessed;" whose ears had just drunk in the glad
tidings of his favorite son, "Joseph is yet alive; he is gov-
ernor over all the land of Egypt." Thus timid and discon-
solate gray hairs bewail their own times. To most men, the
golden age is one long past.

But Nature is ever growing. Science tells us every
change is improvement. This globe, once a mass of molten
granite, now blooms almost a paradise. So in man's life and
history. One may not see it in his own short day. You
must stand afar off to judge St. Peter's. The shadow on
the dial seems motionless, but it touches noon at last. Place
the ages side by side, and see how they differ. Three-quar-
ters of the early kings of France died poor and in prison,
by the dagger or poison of their rivals. The Bonapartes

stole large fortunes and half the thrones of Europe, yet all died natural deaths in their beds, and though discrowned, kept their enormous wealth.

When the English marched from Boston to Concord, they fired into half the Whig dwellings they passed. When Lane crossed Kansas, pursuing Missouri ruffians, he sent men ahead to put a guard at every border ruffian's door, to save inmate and goods from harm. When Goldsmith reminded England that "a heart buried in a dungeon is as precious as that seated on a throne," there were one hundred and sixty-nine crimes punished with death. Now, not only England, but every land governed by the English race, is marked by the mildness of its penal code, only one, two, or three classes of offenders being now murdered by law.

It is not yet fifteen years since the first Woman's Rights Convention was held. The first call for one in Massachusetts, a dozen years ago, bore a name heard often in manful protest against popular sins — that of Waldo Emerson. But in that short fifteen years, a dozen States have changed their laws. One New York statute, a year old, securing to married women control of their wages, will do more to save New York City from being grogshop and brothel than a thousand pulpits could do. When Kansas went to Topeka to frame a constitution, one-third of the Convention were in favor of giving woman the right to vote. Truly, the day breaks. If time served, I could find a score of familiar instances. It is enough to state the general principle, that civilization produces wants. Wants awaken intellect. To gratify them disciplines intellect. The keener the want, the lustier the growth. The power to use new truths in science, new ideas in morals or art, obliterates rank, and makes the lowest man useful or necessary to the State. Luther and Raphael, Fulton and Faust, Howard and Rousseau, mark the ages, not popes or kings. A Massachusetts mechanic, Eli Whitney, made cotton king; a Massachusetts printer, William Lloyd Garrison, has undermined its throne. Thus, civilization insures equality. Types are the fathers of democrats.

It is not always, however, ideas or moral principles that push the world forward. Selfish interests play a large part in the work. Our revolution of 1776 succeeded because trade and wealth joined hands with principle and enthusiasm, a union rare in the history of revolutions. Northern merchants fretted at England's refusal to allow them direct trade with Holland and the West Indies. Virginia planters, heavily mortgaged, welcomed any thing that would postpone payment of their debts—a motive that doubtless avails largely among secessionists now. So merchant and planter joined heartily with hot-headed Sam Adams, and reckless Joseph Warren, penniless John Adams, that brilliant adventurer, Alexander Hamilton, and that young scapegrace, Aaron Burr, to get independence. (Laughter.) To merchant, independence meant only direct trade — to planter, cheating his creditors.

Present conflict of interests is another instrument of progress. Religious persecution planted these States; commercial persecution brought about the Revolution; John Bull's perseverance in a seven years' war fused us into one nation; his narrow and ill-tempered effort to govern us by stealth, even after the peace of 1783, drove us to the Constitution of 1789.

I think it was Coleridge who said, if he were a clergyman in Cornwall, he should preach fifty-two sermons a year against wreckers. In the same spirit, I shall find the best illustration of our progress in the history of the slave question.

Some men sit sad and trembling for the future, because the knell of this Union has sounded. But the heavens are almost all bright; and if some sable clouds linger on the horizon, they have turned their silver linings almost wholly to our sight. Every man who possesses his soul in patience sees that disunion is gain, disunion is *peace*, disunion is virtue.

Thomas Jefferson said, " It is unfortunate that the efforts of mankind to recover the freedom of which they have been deprived should be accompanied with violence, with errors, and even with crime. But while we weep over the means, we must pray for the end."

We may see our future in the glass of our past history. The whole connection of Massachusetts Colony with England was as much disgrace as honor to both sides. On the part of England, it was an attempt to stretch principles which were common sense and justice applied to an island, but absurd and tyrannical applied across the ocean. It was power without right, masked in form. On the side of the

3*

Colony, it was petty shifts, quibbles, equivocations, cunning
dodges, white lies, ever the resource of weakness.   While
England was bull-dog, Massachusetts was fox.   Whoever
cannot take his right openly by force, steals what he can by
fraud.   The Greek slave was a liar, as all slaves are.   De
Tocqueville says, "Men are not corrupted by the exercise
of power, nor debased by submission ; but by the exercise
of power they think illegal, and submission to a rule they
consider oppressive."   That sentence is a key to our whole
colonial history.   When we grew strong enough to dare to
be frank, we broke with England.   Timid men wept ; but
now we see how such disunion was gain, peace, and virtue.
Indeed, seeming disunion was real union.   We were then
two snarling hounds, leashed together ; we are now one in a
true marriage, one in blood, trade, thought, religion, history,
in mutual love and respect ; where one then filched silver
from the other, each now pours gold into the other's lap ;
our only rivalry, which shall do most honor to the blood of
Shakspeare and Milton, of Franklin and Kane.

In that glass we see the story of North and South since
1787, and I doubt not for all coming time.   The people of
the States between the Gulf and the great Lakes, yes,
between the Gulf and the Pole, are essentially one.   We
are one in blood, trade, thought, religion, history ; nothing can long divide us.   If we had let our Constitution
grow, as the English did, as oaks do, we had never passed
through such scenes as the present.   The only thing that
divides us now, is the artificial attempt, in 1787, to force us
into an unripe union.   Some lawyers got together, and
wrote out a Constitution.   The people and great interests
of the land, wealth, thought, fashion, and creed, immediately
laid it upon the shelf, and proceeded to *grow* one for themselves.   The treaty power sufficed to annex a continent, and
change the whole nature of the government.   The war power
builds railroads to the Pacific.   Right to regulate commerce
builds observatories and dredges out lakes.   Right to tax
protects manufactures ; and had we wanted a king, some
ingenious Yankee would have found the right to have one
clearly stated in the provision for a well-regulated militia.
(Laughter.)   All that is valuable in the United States Constitution is a thousand years old.   What is good is not new,
and what is new is not good.   That vaunted statesmanship

which concocts constitutions never has amounted to any thing. The English Constitution, always found equal to any crisis, is an old mansion, often repaired, with quaint additions, and seven gables, each of different pattern. Our Constitution is a new clapboard house, so square and sharp it almost cuts you to look at it, staring with white paint and green blinds, as if dropped in the landscape, or come out to spend an afternoon. (Laughter.)

The trouble now is, that, in regard to the most turbulent question of the age, our politicians and a knot of privileged slaveholders are trying to keep the people inside of this parchment band. Like Lycurgus, they would mould the people to fit the Constitution, instead of cutting the Constitution to fit the people. Goethe said, " If you plant an oak in a flower vase, one of two things will happen — the oak will die, or the vase break." Our acorn swelled ; the tiny leaves showed themselves under the calm eye of Washington, and he laid down in hope. By and by, the roots enlarged, and men trembled. Of late, Webster and Clay, Everett and Botts, Seward and Adams, have been anxiously clasping the vase, but the roots have burst abroad at last, and the porcelain is in pieces. (Sensation.) All ye who love oaks, thank God for so much! That Union of 1787 was one of fear ; we were driven into it by poverty and the commercial hostility of England. As cold masses up all things, — sticks earth, stones, and water into dirty ice, — heat first makes separation, and then unites those of the same nature. The heat of sixty years' agitation has severed the heterogeneous mass; wait awhile, it will fuse together all that is really one.

Let me show you why I think the present so bright, and why I believe that disunion is gain, peace, and honor.

Why is the present hour sunshine ? Because, for the first time in our history, we have a North. That event which Mr. Webster anticipated and prophesied has come to pass. In a real, true sense, we have a North. By which I do not mean that the North rules, though, politically speaking, the crowned and sceptred North does, indeed, take her seat in that council where she has thus far been only a tool. But I mean that free men, honest labor, makes itself heard in our State. The North ceases to be fox or spaniel, and puts on the lion. She asserts and claims. She no longer begs, cheats, or buys.

Understand me. In 1787, slave property, worth, perhaps, two hundred million of dollars, strengthened by the sympathy of all other capital, was a mighty power. It was the Rothschild of the State. The Constitution, by its *three-fifths slave basis*, made slaveholders an order of nobles. It was the house of Hapsburg joining hands with the house of Rothschild. Prejudice of race was the third strand of the cable, bitter and potent as Catholic ever bore Huguenot, or Hungary ever spit on Moslem. This fearful trinity won to its side that mysterious omnipotence called *Fashion* — a power which, without concerted action, without either thought, law, or religion on its side, seems stronger than all of them, and fears no foe but wealth. Such was slavery. In its presence the North always knelt and whispered. When slavery could not bully, it bubbled its victim. In the convention that framed the Constitution, Massachusetts men said, as Charles Francis Adams says now, " What matters a pitiful three-fifths slave basis, and guarantee against insurrection, to an institution on its death-bed — gasping for its last breath ? It may *conciliate* — is only a shadow — nothing more — why stand on words ? " So they shut their eyes, as he does, on realities, and chopped excellent logic on forms.

But at that moment, the Devil hovered over Charleston, with a handful of cotton-seed. (Applause.) Dropped into sea-island soil, and touched by the magic of Massachusetts brains, it poisoned the atmosphere of thirty States. That cotton fibre was a rod of empire such as Cæsar never wielded. It fattened into obedience pulpit and rostrum, court, market-place and college, and leashed New York and Chicago to its chair of State. Beware, Mr. Adams, " he needs a long spoon who sups with the Devil." In the kaleidoscope of the future, no statesman eye can foresee the forms. God gives narrow manhood but one clue to success — utter and exact justice ; that he guarantees shall be always expediency. Deviate one hair's-breath — grant but a dozen slaves — only the tiniest seed of concession — you know not how " many and tall branches of mischief shall grow therefrom." That handful of cotton-seed has perpetuated a system which, as Emerson says, " impoverishes the soil, depopulates the country, demoralizes the master, curses the victim, enrages the bystander, poisons the atmosphere, and hinders civilization."

I need not go over the subsequent compromises in detail. They are always of the same kind : mere words, Northern men assured us — barren concessions. "Physical geography and Asiatic scenery" hindered any harm. But the South was always specially anxious to have these barren " words," and marvellously glad when she got them. Northern politicians, in each case, were either bullied or cheated, or feigned to be bullied, as they are about to do now. And the people were glad to have it so. I do not know that the politicians *are* a whit better now than then. I should not be willing to assert that Seward and Adams are any more honest than Webster and Winthrop, and certainly they have just as much spaniel in their make.

But the gain to-day is, we have a *people*. Under their vigilant eyes, mindful of their sturdy purpose, sustained by their determination, many of our politicians *act* much better. And out of this popular heart is *growing* a Constitution which will wholly supersede that of 1787.

A few years ago, while Pierce was President, the Republican party dared to refuse the appropriations for support of government — the most daring act ever ventured in a land that holds Bunker Hill and Brandywine. They dared to persevere some twenty or thirty days. It seems a trifle; but it is a very significant straw. Then for weeks when Banks was elected, and a year ago, again, the whole government was checked till the Republicans put their Speaker in the chair. Now the North elects her President, the South secedes. I suppose we shall be bargained away into compromise. I know the strength and virtue of the farming West. It is one of the bright spots that our sceptre tends there, rather than to the seaboard. Four or eight years hence, when this earthquake will repeat itself, the West may be omnipotent, and we shall see brave things. It is not the opinion of the absolute majority that rules, but that amount of public opinion which can be brought to bear on a particular point at a given time. Therefore the compact, energetic, organized Seaboard, with the press in its hand, rules spite of the wide-spread, inert, unorganized West. While the agricultural frigate is getting its broadside ready, the commercial clipper has half finished its slave voyage.

In spite of Lincoln's wishes, therefore, I fear he will never be able to stand against Seward, Adams, half the Republican wire-pullers and the seaboard. But even now, if Seward and the rest had stood firm, as Lincoln, Sumner, Chase, Wade, and Lovejoy, and the *Tribune* have hitherto done, I believe you might have polled the North, and had a response, three to one, " Let the Union go to pieces, rather than yield one inch." I know no sublimer hour in history. The sight of these two months is compensation for a life of toil. Never let Europe taunt us again that our blood is wholly cankered by gold. Our people stood, willing their idolized government should go to pieces for an idea. True, other nations have done so. England in 1640 — France in 1791 — our colonies in 1775. Those were proud moments. But to-day touches a nobler height. Their idea was their own freedom. To-day, the idea, loyal to which our people willingly see their Union wrecked, is largely the hope of justice to a dependent, helpless, hated race. Revolutions never go backward. The live force of a human pulse-beat can rive the dead lumber of government to pieces. Chain the Hellespont, Mr. Xerxes-Seward, before you dream of balking the Northern heart of its purpose — freedom to the slave! The old sea never laughed at Persian chains more haughtily than we do at Congress-compromises.

I reverently thank God that he has given me to see such a day as this. Remember the measureless love of the North for the Union, — its undoubting faith that disunion is ruin, — and then value as you ought this last three months. If Wilberforce could say on his death-bed, after fifty years' toil, " Thank God, I have lived to see the day that England is willing to give twenty million sterling for the abolition of slavery," what ought our gratitude to be for such a sight as this? Twenty millions of people willing, would only their leaders permit, to barter their government for the hope of justice to the negro ! And this result has come in defiance of the pulpit, spite of the half omnipotence of commerce, with all the so-called leaders of public opinion against us — literature, fashion, prejudice of race, and present interest. It is the uprising of common sense, the protest of common conscience, the untaught, instinctive loyalty of the people to justice and right.

But you will tell me of dark clouds, mobs in every Northern city. Grant it, and more. When Lovejoy was shot, at Alton, Illinois, while defending his press, and Faneuil Hall was closed to his friends, William Ellery Channing, William Sturgis, and George Bond, the saints and merchants of Boston, rallied to the defence of free speech. Now, we hold meetings only when and how the mayor permits (hisses and great applause), yet no merchant prince, no pulpit hero rallies to our side. But raise your eyes from the disgraced pavements of Boston, and look out broader. That same soil which drank the blood of Lovejoy, now sends his brother to lead Congress in its fiercest hour; that same prairie lifts his soul's son to crush the Union as he steps into the presidential chair. Sleep in peace, martyr of Alton, good has come out of Nazareth! The shot which turned back our Star of the West from the waters of Charleston, and tolled the knell of the Union, was the rebound of the bullet that pierced your heart.

When Lovejoy died, men used to ask, tauntingly, what good has the anti-slavery cause done? what changes has it wrought? As well stand over the cradle, and ask what use is a baby? He will be a man some time — the anti-slavery cause is now twenty-one years old.

This hour is bright from another cause. Since 1800, our government has been only a tool of the Slave Power. The stronghold of anti-slavery has been the sentiment of the people. We have always prophesied that our government would be found too weak to bear so radical an agitation as this of slavery. It has proved so; the government is a wreck. But the people have shown themselves able to deal with it—able to shake this sin from their lap as easily as the lion does dewdrops from his mane.

Mark another thing. No Northern man will allow you to charge him with a willingness to extend slavery. No matter what his plan, he is anxious to show you it is not a compromise! and will not extend slavery one inch! Mr. Dana is eloquent on this point, Mr. Adams positive, Mr. Seward cunning, Thurlow Weed indignant. (Laughter.) Virtue is not wholly discrowned, while hypocrisy is the homage laid at her feet. With such progress, why should we compromise?

Everybody allows — North and South — that any compromise will only be temporary relief. The South knows it is a lie, meant to tide over a shallow spot. The North knows it, too. The startled North, in fact, now says: "Yes, I'll continue to serve you till my hair be grown, then I'll bring down the very temple itself." That is what a compromise really means. The progress is seen in this. The South always has said: "Yes, give me so much; I will not keep my part of the bargain, but hold you to yours, and get more the moment I can." Hitherto the North has said yes, and her courage consisted in skulking. Seward would *swear* to support the Constitution, but not to keep the oath. I use his name to illustrate my idea. But it is always with the extremest reluctance I bring myself to see a spot on the fame of that man, who, at his own cost, by severe toil, braving fierce odium, saved our civilization from the murder of the idiot Freeman.

But you may also ask, if compromise be even a temporary relief, why not make it?

1st, Because it is wrong.

2d, Because it is suicidal. Secession, appeased by compromise, is only emboldened to secede again to-morrow, and thus get larger concessions. The cowardice that yields to threats invites them.

3d, Because it delays emancipation. To-day, England, horror-struck that her five million operatives who live on cotton should depend on States rushing into anarchy, is ransacking the world for a supply. Leave her to toil under that lash, and in five years, South Carolina will be starved into virtue. One thousand slaves are born each day. Hurry emancipation three years, and you raise a million human beings into freeborn men.

4th, Compromise demoralizes both parties. Mark! the North, notwithstanding all its progress, does not now quit the South. In the great religious bodies and the State, it is the sinners who kick the virtuous out of the covenant with death! Mr. Dana, in his recent speech, does not secede because unwilling to commit the three constitutional sins. The South secedes from him because he will not commit one more.

5th, Compromise risks insurrection, the worst door at which freedom can enter. · Let universal suffrage have free sway, and the ballot supersedes the bullet. But let an arrogant and besotted minority curb the majority by tricks like these, and when you have compromised away Lincoln, you revive John Brown. On this point of insurrection, let me say a word.

Strictly speaking, I repudiate the term "insurrection." The slaves are not a herd of vassals. They are a nation, four millions strong; having the same right of revolution that Hungary and Florence have. I acknowledge the right of two million and a half of white people in the seven seceding states to organize their government as they choose. Just as freely I acknowledge the right of four million of black people to organize *their* government, and to vindicate that right by arms.

Men talk of the peace of the South under our present government. It is no real peace. With the whites, it is only that bastard peace which the lazy Roman loved,— *ut se apricaret,* — that he might sun himself. It is only safe idleness, sure breeder of mischief. With the slave, it is only war in disguise. Under that mask is hid a war keener in its pains, and deadlier in its effects, than any open fight. As the Latin adage runs, — *mars gravior sub pace latet,* — war bitterer for its disguise.

Thirty years devoted to earnest use of moral means show how sincere our wish that this question should have a peaceful solution. If your idols — your Websters, Clays, Calhouns, Sewards, Adamses — had done their duty, so it would have been. Not ours the guilt of this storm, or of the future, however bloody. But I hesitate not to say that I prefer an insurrection which frees the slave in ten years to slavery for a century. A slave I pity. A rebellious slave I respect. I say now, as I said ten years ago, I do not shrink from the toast with which Dr. Johnson flavored his Oxford port. "Success to the first insurrection of the blacks in Jamaica!" I do not shrink from the sentiment of Southey, in a letter to Duppa, "There are scenes of tremendous horror which I could smile at by Mercy's side. An insurrection which should make the negroes masters of the West Indies is one." I believe both these sentiments are dictated by the highest humanity. I know what an-

4

archy is. I know what civil war is. I can imagine the scenes of blood through which a rebellious slave population must march to their rights. They are dreadful. And yet, I do not know, that, to an enlightened mind, a scene of civil war is any more sickening than the thought of a hundred and fifty years of slavery. Take the broken hearts; the bereaved mothers; the infant, wrung from the hands of its parents; the husband and wife torn asunder; every right trodden under foot; the blighted hopes, the imbruted souls, the darkened and degraded millions, sunk below the level of intellectual life, melted in sensuality, herded with beasts, who have walked over the burning marl of Southern slavery to their graves; and where is the battle-field, however ghastly, that is not white,—white as an angel's wing,—compared with the blackness of that darkness which has brooded over the Carolinas for two hundred years? Do you love mercy? Weigh out the fifty thousand hearts that have beaten their last pulse amid agonies of thought and suffering fancy faints to think of; and the fifty thousand mothers, who, with sickening senses, watch for footsteps that are not wont to tarry long in their coming, and soon find themselves left to tread the pathway of life alone; add all the horrors of cities sacked and lands laid waste, — that is war, — weigh it now against some trembling young girl sent to the auction-block, some man, like that taken from our courthouse and carried back into Georgia; multiply this individual agony into four millions; multiply that into centuries; and that into all the relations of father and child, husband and wife; heap on all the deep, moral degradation both of the oppressor and the oppressed, and tell me if Waterloo or Thermopylæ can claim one tear from the eye even of the tenderest spirit of mercy, compared with this daily system of hell amid the most civilized and Christian people on the face of the earth ! *

* Macaulay makes the same comparison between a short civil war and long despotism — putting into Milton's mouth the following: "For civil war that it is an evil I dispute not. But that it is the greatest of evils, that I stoutly deny. It doth indeed appear to the misjudging to be a worse calamity than bad government, because its miseries are collected together within a short space and time, and may easily, at one view, be taken in and perceived. But the misfortunes of nations, ruled by tyrants, being distributed over many centuries and many places, as they are of greater weight and number, so they are of less display."

No, I confess I am not a non-resistant. The reason why I have advised the slave to be guided by a policy of peace is because he has had, hitherto, no chance. If he had one, if he had as good a chance as those who went up to Lexington years ago, I should call him the basest recreant that ever deserted wife and child, if he did not vindicate his liberty by his own right hand.

Mr. Richard H. Dana, Jr., says in such a contest his sympathies would be with his own race.* I confess mine would be with the right. I feel bound to add my doubt whether a slave insurrection would be a bloody one. In all revolutions, except the French, the people have always shown themselves merciful. Witness Switzerland, St. Domingo, Hungary, Italy. Tyranny sours more than suffering. The Conservative hates the Abolitionist more than we do him. The South hates the North. The master speaks ten bitter words of the slave where the slave speaks five of the master. Refuse all compromise — send the Slave States out to face the danger of which they are fully aware — announce frankly that we welcome the black race to liberty, won in battle, as cordially as we have done Kossuth and Garibaldi, and probably there will never be an insurrection. Prudent and masterly statesmanship will avert it by just concession. Thus Disunion is Peace as well as Liberty and Justice.

But I was speaking of compromise. Compromise degrades us, and puts back freedom in Europe. If the North manfully accepts the Potomac for her barrier, avows her glad-

---

* The following is the paragraph in Mr. Dana's address, referred to by Mr. Phillips :—

"An appeal to arms is a war of the races. They meet on the equality of the battle-field, and the victory goes to the strongest; and I confess that, when I consider what the white race is, and what the black race is, what civilization is, and what the white race is and always has been, and what the black race is and always has been,— and this doctrine of the races has impressed itself on my mind much more than before, from what I have seen of all races during the last year and a half,—I confess that, in a contest like that, my duty and my sympathies would go with my own race. I know it is a contest for freedom, but it is a contest for life and for freedom on both sides, because *slavery is to end when war begins.* One race is to go up, and one to go down. It is a question of extermination, or banishment, or subjugation, or all three. And I have not arrived at that degree of philanthropy that I desire to see the black race controlling all that vast country, and our own white civilized race driven out, subjugated, or exterminated."

ness to get rid of tyrants, her willingness and her ability to stand alone, she can borrow as much money in Europe as before, and will be more respected. Free institutions are then proved breeders of men. If, instead of this, the North belittles herself by confessing her fears, her weakness, her preference for peace at any price, what capitalist will trust a rope of sand — a people which the conspiracy of Buchanan's Cabinet could not disgust, nor the guns of Carolina arouse?

Will compromise eliminate all our Puritan blood — make the census add up against us and in favor of the South — write a new Testament — blot John Brown from history — make Connecticut suck its idle thumbs like a baby, and South Carolina invent and save like a Yankee? If it will, it will succeed. If it will not, Carolina don't want it any more than Jerrold's duck wants you to hold an umbrella over him in a hard shower. Carolina wants separation — wants, like the jealous son, her portion, and must waste it in riotous madness before she return a repentant prodigal.

Why do I think disunion gain, peace, and virtue?

The Union, even if it be advantageous to all the States, is surely indispensable only to the South.

Let us rise to the height of our position. This is revolution, not rebellion.

Suppose we welcome disunion, manfully avow our real sentiment, "liberty and equality," and draw the line at the Potomac. We do not want the Border States. Let them go, be welcome to the forts, take the Capitol with them. (Applause and hisses.) What to us is a hot-house city, empty streets, and useless marble? Where Macgregor sits is the head of the table. Active brains, free lips, and cunning hands make empires. Paper Capitals are vain. Of course, we must assume a right to buy out Maryland and Delaware. Then, by running our line at the Potomac, we close the irrepressible conflict, and have homogeneous institutions. Then we part friends. The Union thus ended, the South no longer hates the North. Cuba she cannot have. France, England, and ourselves forbid. If she spread over Central America, that will bring no cause of war to a Northern confederacy. We are no fillibusters. Her nearness to us there cannot harm us. Let Kansas witness that while Union fettered her, and our national banner clung to the flag-staff heavy with blood, we still made good George Canning's boast, "Where that banner is planted, foreign dominion shall not come." With a government heartily on his side, and that flag floating in the blessings of twenty million of freemen, the loneliest settler in the shadow of the Rocky Mountains will sleep fearless.

Why, then, should there not be peace between two such confederacies? There must be. Let me show you why:—

1st, The laws of trade will bind us together as they now do all other lands. This side of the ocean, at least, we are not living in feudal times, when princes made war for ambition. We live in days when men of common sense go about their daily business, while frightened kings are flying along the highways. Leave neighborhood and trade alone to work their usual results, and we shall be at peace. Observe, only Northerners are lynched at the South now. Spaniards, French, Scotch are safe. When English Captain Vaughan is tarred and feathered, the mayor offers a reward, and the grand jury indict. After a fair, sensible disunion, such as I have described, a Boston man will be as well off as Captain Vaughan. Fair Treaties are better security than sham Constitutions.

At any rate, disunion could not make the two sections any more at war than they are now. Any change in this respect would be an improvement. If the North and Mexico had touched boundaries, would they ever have quarrelled? Nothing but Southern fillibusterism, which can never point North, ever embroiled us with Mexico. To us in future the South will be another Mexico; we shall not wish to attack her; she will be too weak, too intent on her own broils, to attack us.

Even if the Border States do not secede, let us, for the slave's sake, welcome the schism between them and the Gulf States, which that very difference of conduct will be sure to cause. A house divided against itself cannot stand. Only twenty-three out of every hundred inhabitants are slaves in the Border States—twenty-three slaves to seventy-seven freemen. Fear of loss by fugitives, dread of danger to a hated institution, thus weak in proportion to Northern enemies, will urge slaveholders to push their slaves Southward. Another census may find the Border States with only ten or fifteen slaves out of one hundred inhabitants — ten slaves to ninety freemen. Reduced to such compass

4*

slavery is manageable; we shall soon see plans of emancipation, compensation, and freedom. On the contrary, the
Gulf States now have forty-six slaves in every hundred inhabitants — forty-six slaves to fifty-four freemen. Strengthened by this tendency of the slave population Southward,
and the opening of the slave-trade, we may soon see the
black race a majority, and either as a nation of mixed races,
or as black republics, the Gulf States will gravitate back to
us *free*.

The South cannot make war on any one. Suppose the
fifteen States hang together a year, — which is almost an
impossibility, — 1st, they have given bonds in two thousand
million of dollars — the value of their slaves — to keep the
peace.

2d, They will have enough to do to attend to the irrepressible conflict at home. Virginia, Kentucky, Missouri, will
be their Massachusetts; Winter Davis, Blair, and Cassius
Clay, their Seward and Garrison.

3d, The Gulf States will monopolize all the offices. A
man must have Gulf principles to belong to a healthy party.
Under such a lead, disfranchised Virginia, in opposition,
will not have much heart to attack Pennsylvania.

4th, The census shows that the Border States are push-
ing their slaves south. Fear of their free Northern neigh-
bors will quicken the process, and so widen the breach between Gulf and Border States by making one constantly
more and the other less Slave States. Free trade in sugar
bankrupts Louisiana. Free trade in men bankrupts Virginia.
Free trade generally lets two-thirds of the direct taxation
rest on the numerous, richer, and more comfortable whites
of the Border States; hence further conflict. Such a despotism, with every third man black and a foe, will make no
wars.

Why should it attack us? We are not a cannon thun-
dering at its gates. We are not an avalanche overhanging
its sunny vales. Our influence, that of freedom, is only the
air, penetrating everywhere; like heat, permeating all space.
The South cannot stand isolated on a glass cricket. The
sun will heat her, and electricity convulse. She must out-
wit them before she can get rid of ideas. A fevered child
in July might as well strike at the sun, as the South attack

us for that, the only annoyance we can give her, — the sight and influence of our nobler civilization.

Disunion is gain. I venture the assertion, in the face of State Street, that of any five Northern men engaged in Southern trade exclusively, four will end in bankruptcy. If disunion sifts such commerce, the North will lose nothing.

I venture the assertion, that seven at least of the Southern States receive from the government more than they contribute to it. So far, their place will be more profitable than their company.

The whole matter of the Southern trade has been grossly exaggerated, as well as the importance of the Mississippi River. Freedom makes her own rivers of iron. Facts show that for one dollar the West sends or brings by the river, she sends and brings four to and from the East by wagon and rail.

If, then, Mississippi and Louisiana bar the river with forts, they will graciously be allowed to pay for them, while Northern railroads grow rich carrying behind steam that portion of wheat, bacon, silk, or tea, which would otherwise float lazily up and down that yellow stream.

The Cincinnati *Press*, which has treated this subject with rare ability, asserts that, excepting provisions which the South must, in any event, buy of the West, the trade of Cincinnati with Southern Indiana alone is thrice her trade with the whole South. As our benevolent societies get about one dollar in seven south of Mason and Dixon's line, so our traders sell there only about one dollar in five. Such trade, if cut off, would ruin nobody. In fact, the South buys little of us, and pays only for about half she buys. (Laughter and hisses.)

Now we build Southern roads, pay Southern patrol, carry Southern letters, support, out of the nation's treasures, an army of Southern office-holders, waste more money at Norfolk in building ships that will not float, than is spent in protecting the five great lakes, which bear up millions of commerce. These vast pensions come back to us in shape of Southern traders, paying, on the average, one-half their debts. Dissolve the Union, and we shall save this outgo, and probably not sell without a prospect of being paid. While the laws of trade guarantee that even if there be two nations, we shall have their carrying trade and manufacture for them just so long as we carry and manufacture cheaper than other men.

Southern trade is a lottery, to which the Union gives all the prizes. Put it on a sound basis by disunion, and the North gains. If we part without anger, the South buys, as • every one does, of the cheapest seller. We get her honest business, without being called to fill up the gap of bankruptcy which the wasteful system of slave-labor must occasion. In this generation, no Slave State in the Union has made the year's ends meet. In counting the wealth of the Union, such States are a *minus* quantity. Should the Gulf States, however, return, I have no doubt the United States treasury will be called on to pay all these secession debts.

Disunion is honor. I will not count up all the bankrupt statesmen — blighted names — skeletons marking the sad path of the caravan over our desert of seventy years — they are too familiar. As years roll on, history metes out justice. But take the last instance — take Mr. Richard H. Dana, Jr., as example, a name historic for generations, a scholar of worldwide fame. He finds in the Constitution the duty of returning fugitive slaves, all alike, "the old and the ignorant, the young and the beautiful," to be surrendered to the master, whether he be man or brute. Mr. Dana avows his full readiness to perform this legal duty. All honor at least to the shameless effrontery with which he avows his willingness. Most of our public men, like the English Tories of 1689, are "ashamed to name what they are not ashamed to do." He paints the hell of slavery in words that make the blood cold, and then boasts, this Massachusetts scholar — gentleman, his friends would call him — boasts that no man can charge him with having ever said one word against the surrender of fugitive slaves! Counsel in all the Boston slave cases, he "never suffered himself to utter one word which any poor fugitive negro, or any friend of his, could construe into an assertion that a fugitive slave should not be restored!"

He unblushingly claims merit for himself and Massachusetts — I doubt if, in the scornful South, he will have "his claim allowed" — that he and Massachusetts have constantly executed laws which "offended their sense of honor, and ran counter to their moral sentiments," which he considers a " painful *duty.*" To be sure, Mr. Dana has discovered in his wide travels and extensive voyages a "peculiar" class of people, narrow-minded, very little read in Greek, who think, poor simpletons, that this slave-hunting is a sin. But then, Aristotle did not look at things in this light. He took broader views, and proves conclusively that three virtues and one sin exactly make a saint, and Mr. Dana is too good a churchman to dispute with Aristotle. He sees no reason why, notwithstanding this clause as to forcing our fellow-men back into hell, "a conscientious man" should not swear to obey the Constitution, and actually obey it. Now Mr. Seward and Mr. Joel Parker, who both believe in the fugitive slave clause, and willingly *swear* to enforce it, have each given public notice they will not enforce it. Mr. Dana will swear, and perform too. They will swear, but not perform. Their guilt is perjury; his is man-stealing. On the whole, I should rather be Seward than Dana; for perjury is the more gentlemanly vice, to my thinking. Perjury only filches your neighbor's rights. Man-stealing takes rights and neighbor too.

After all this, Mr. Dana objects to the Crittenden compromise. Something short of that he can allow, because he does not call these other offers, Adams' and such like, "compromises"! It seems he objects more to the word than the thing. But the Crittenden proposal he is set against for a reason which may strike you singular in a man willing to return slaves; but then we are bundles of inconsistencies, all of us. But this slave-hunter cannot abide Crittenden because, listen! because he thinks "an investment in dishonor is a bad investment! An investment in infidelity to the principles of liberty is a bad investment!" Hunt slaves? Yes, it is a duty. Give some territory to slavery, and peril the Republican party? Never, it is a "bad investment!" De Quincey says: "If once a man indulges in murder, very soon he comes to think little of robbing; from robbing he comes next to drinking, and from that to ill manners and procrastination. Once enter this downward path, and you know not where you'll stop." Mr. Dana has, however, taken warning, and stops at man-stealing.

Some of you will call this personality. I will tell you some time, when the hour serves, why I use personality. Enough now to remind you his clients are wealth, culture, power, and white blood. Mine are four million of human beings, standing dumb suppliants on the threshold of Christianity and civilization, and hundreds of fugitives trembling at every motion of the door-latch. Whoever perils their safety, or holds back the day of their redemption by ingenious sophistry, base word, or base act, shall always find in me a critic. Let no man call me harsh; I only *repeat* with emphasis words such men are not ashamed to *speak.* Southern Legrees can plead, if not excuse, yet some extenuation. But when a Massachusetts Republican, a Massachusetts lawyer, a Massachusetts scholar avows such sentiments, he puts himself below the Legrees. Blame not this plainness of speech. I have a hundred friends, as brave souls as God ever made, whose hearths are not as safe after honored men make such speeches.

Faneuil Hall, too, kneels patient for its burden, and by its president that meeting says to the South, "Only name your terms, that is all we will trouble you to do." Like Luther's priest, who, when Catholics told him to pray one way and Protestants another, ended by repeating the alphabet, and begging God to frame a prayer agreeable to himself, so our Boston orator offers the South *carte blanche*, the whole bundle of compromises; "will she only condescend to indicate her preference?"

Mr. Dana is a man above the temptations of politics. The president of the Faneuil Hall meeting has no political aspirations, an independent gentleman. Such speeches show how wide the gangrene of the Union spreads. Mr. Dana's speech was made, he says, in the shadow of Bunker's Hill, in sight of the spot where Washington first drew his sword. The other speech was borne to the roof of Faneuil Hall by the plaudits of a thousand merchants. Surely, such were not the messages Cambridge and our old Hall used to exchange! Can you not hear Warren and Otis crying to their recreant representatives: "Sons, scorn to be slaves! Believe, for our sakes, we did not fight for such a government. Trample it under foot. You cannot be poorer than we were. It cannot cost you more than our seven years of war. Do it, if only to show that we have not lived in vain."

www.ingramcontent.com/pod-product-compliance
Lightning Source LLC
Chambersburg PA
CBHW032133080426
42733CB00008B/1047